THE OLD STEAM TRAIN

M. G. Leonard

Illustrated by Alex Shurety

Ernst Klett Sprachen
Stuttgart

Augmented

You can access the audiobook on your mobile phone or a tablet. Download and install the Klett Augmented app.

Scan the title page (p 1) using the camera on your mobile phone/tablet. Then download the audio files for each chapter.

| Install the Klett Augmented app on your device | Open the app on your device and select the cover | Start picture recognition and scan the title page | Download files and use them straight away or save them for later |

Apple und das Apple-Logo sind Marken der Apple Inc., die in den USA und weiteren Ländern eingetragen sind. App Store ist eine Dienstleistungsmarke der Apple Inc. | Google Play und das Google Play-Logo sind Marken der Google Inc.

Bookmark*

The bookmark can help you with difficult words. These words are marked with * in the text.
In case you lose the bookmark, you can download it again at *www.klett-sprachen.de* by entering the following code in the search field: **gznye3m**

Contents

Team Read

Choose one of the following characters and tick the box. Read only your character's chapters and those chapters that *everybody* has to read.

Of course ...

You *can* always read the whole story and discover everything that's going on for yourself!

Read chapters for :
1, 2, 5, 8, 9, 10, 13, 14, 15, 16

GEORGE

Choose to follow George if you do not read books very often or if you feel that long texts in English are confusing. George has a secret! But what is it? Can you find out why he spends so much time at the junkyard?

> Read chapters for Ⓒ:
> 1, 2, 3, 6, 9, 10, 11, 14, 15, 16

CLAIRE

Claire discovered an old steam train in the junkyard – so she thinks. If you sometimes read books *or* if English isn't really difficult for you, follow Claire's chapters. Is she really serious about hunting ghosts?

> Read chapters for Ⓡ:
> 1, 2, 4, 7, 9, 10, 12, 14, 15, 16

ROSIE

Rosie does some research on steam trains – and finds out more about Old Ned. If you read a lot *or* if English is really easy for you, read Rosie's chapters. Dig into the past, learn more about steam trains and find out about the tragic accident that changed Old Ned's life.

1 The Discovery

'Hey, Rosie!' Claire yelled* as she ran across the grass towards the playground. Her brown hair flew out behind her, and her face was a picture of delight*. Her blue eyes were shining and she was grinning* wide as she sprinted towards the pale* girl who sat on the swing*. 'You'll never guess what I've found?'

Rosie was Claire's best friend. Their mums were best friends. They had known each other since they were babies. Rosie's younger brother, George, a thin blond boy with grey eyes like his sister's, was standing on the swing next to his sister, rocking backwards and forwards.

'What is it?' Rosie stood up as Claire bounced across the playground.

'I've found the most wonderful thing,' Claire put her hands on her knees as she paused to catch her breath, 'I was exploring the junkyard*...'

'What did you go there for?' George asked, jumping down from the swing.

'We have to make a robot for our art homework,' Claire replied. 'I wanted to see if I could find some bits of metal to use.'

'Good idea!' Rosie said. 'I made mine from cardboard* boxes and toilet rolls. It looks rubbish.'

George nodded*. 'It does.'

'Hey!' Rosie pulled* a face at her brother and George laughed.

'Old Ned wasn't there,' Claire said.

'You shouldn't go into the junkyard if Old Ned isn't there,' George said. 'It's dangerous.'

'I know, but I was only poking* about looking for small bits and bobs*,' Claire replied.

'I still don't think you should've gone in,' George said.

Claire leaned* forwards. 'You'll never guess what I found. Right at the back, if you go around Old Ned's cabin* and over the bonnet* of a yellow car, there's a path between the mountains of junk. If you follow it to the end there are big wooden doors. They've got a padlock* on them, so naturally I was curious*...'

'What did you find?' Rosie asked, pushing her flyaway hair back from her face and tucking it behind her ear.

'I only saw a part of it,' Claire said, her eyes sparkling*. 'The padlock on the door stopped me from opening it any wider than an inch, but it looked like an old steam* engine.'

'A what?' Rosie frowned*.

'It's huge,' Claire said.

'That's impossible*,' George said. 'How would a steam engine get into Old Ned's junkyard?'

'I don't know, but it is there. If you don't believe me, come back with me and I'll show you.'

'A steam engine?' Rosie stared at Claire. 'A real old steam engine?'

Claire nodded. 'It's rusty*, but it is a steam train, and there's a carriage* too.'

'I want to see.' Rosie turned to George. 'Let's go and look.'

George shook* his head. 'Mum said we have to be back home for dinner at six o'clock.'

'It's only five o'clock now,' Claire said. 'We can easily get to the junkyard and back before then.

G C R

Perhaps Old Ned will be back.
We can ask him about the train.
Maybe he'll show it to us.
He must have a key to that
padlock.'

Rosie nodded. Claire grabbed her hand and they ran excitedly across the field. 'Aren't you coming George?' Rosie called over her shoulder. 'You love trains.'

'Trains are for nerds,' George shouted back.

'C'mon* then, nerd,' Rosie laughed.

George shook his head, but after a minute, he ran after them.

2 The Ghost Keeper

'Hey, wait for me,' George said, catching*
up with Claire and Rosie. 'What's the rush*?'
He gasped*.

'I want you guys to see it,' Claire replied.
'And you said you had to be home before six.
Wait till you see it. It looks fantastic. I bet* you
there's a story there! What's it doing in Ned's
shed*?'

'If there is a steam train in Old Ned's junkyard,
and no one knows about it, maybe it's a secret*,'
George said. 'Maybe he doesn't want anyone to
know it's there.'

'*Rubbish!* Secrets always get found out in the
end and who would want to keep a steam train
a secret?' Claire said, pulling at his arm as they
swung* open the park gate and stepped* out
onto the pavement*.

'I don't want to go to the junkyard,' George said.

'Why not?' Rosie frowned. 'You love it there.'

'Not anymore I don't.' George looked at the ground and frowned.

'Why?' Claire asked. 'What happened?'

'I don't know if I should tell you this,' George looked at Claire and then his sister, 'because it might frighten* you.'

'Ha! Nothing frightens me.' Claire folded her arms.

'I'm warning you.' George looked serious*. 'There's a story going around about Old Ned and his junkyard. Ever since I heard it, I've stayed away from there and you should too.'

'What's the story about?' Rosie asked, curious.

'The junkyard is haunted*,' George said in a whisper.

'Don't be silly,' Claire laughed. 'I don't believe in ghosts.'

'It's true,' George cried. 'It's haunted and Old Ned is the keeper* of the ghosts.'

'What do you mean, *the keeper of the ghosts*?'
Rosie wasn't laughing. 'Why would Old Ned want
to keep ghosts?'

'I don't know. He's like, their friend. He calls to
dead people's spirits* and the ghosts dance and
whirl* around the junkyard at night time. And
when there's a full moon, they're super scary.'

'There's a full moon tonight,' Rosie said, her eyes growing wide.

'Exactly,' George nodded. 'When I heard that story, I stopped going there.'

'That is the most stupid story I've ever heard,' Claire said, shaking her head. 'Old Ned is nice.'

'Is he?' George asked, suddenly very serious. 'What do you know about him?'

Rosie and Claire looked at each other and shrugged*.

'Not much,' Claire admitted*.

'Do you know what he did before he had the junkyard?'

'No and neither* do you,' Rosie said, scowling at her little brother.

'I do. He was in prison and before that he worked at a funeral* parlour.'

'Woah!' Claire blinked*. 'He was in prison?'

George nodded.

'How do you know that?' Rosie scoffed*.

'Everyone knows. It's part of the story going around.'

'I haven't heard any story,' Claire said, less certain*.

'Have you noticed that Old Ned has no family?' George crossed his arms. 'He hasn't got a wife, or kids, or parents. Why is that?'

'He killed them?' Rosie whispered.

George shrugged. 'All I know is that Old Ned is a ghost keeper and tonight is a full moon, so we should keep* away from the junkyard.'

'If Old Ned is a ghost keeper and there's an old steam train hidden deep within the junkyard,' Claire's eyes flashed, 'I want to go there more than ever.'

George sighed*. 'Don't say I didn't warn you.'

Claire crept* up to the gates of the junkyard. Rosie was two steps behind her. George hung back. There was a thick chain* holding the gates together. Claire tried to pull it. 'It's locked*,' she huffed, disappointed.

Rosie peered* through the gates. 'I don't see a train or any place a train could hide.'

'I promise it's there, round the back of Old Ned's cabin.'

'What's that?' George went rigid* and pointed. 'Something moved. I thought I saw a...' He screamed and ran.

Rosie panicked, screamed and ran after him.

Alarmed, Claire followed them, her heart beating fast. She looked back over her shoulder but saw nothing.

3 A Pale Face

As Claire ate her dinner, she thought about the steam train and George's story about Old Ned. She was angry with herself for getting spooked by the story. George was nearly two years younger than her, of course he'd got frightened. She didn't believe in ghosts, and that train was too good to sit rusting* in an old shed. She quickly ate her dinner of shepherd's pie and peas, chewing and swallowing* as fast as she could.

'Slow down or you'll choke*,' her mother said, laughing.

'Mum, Dad, I need to pop* out after dinner,' Claire said. 'There's something I need to do.'

'It's getting late, love,' said her mother, looking out the window at the setting sun.

'I know, but I won't be long – just twenty minutes. I have to collect six different types of leaf* for my Biology homework.'

'Can't you do that in the morning?'

'No, because then I also need to write about them,' Claire lied.

'Well, as long as you're back before it gets dark,' her father said.

'Thanks, I'll be quick.' Claire pushed her chair back from the table and hurried into the hall. She grabbed her coat, calling goodbye as she yanked* the front door open. Once outside, she scurried* back to Old Ned's junkyard.

The more she thought about it, the more she believed George and Rosie were being silly. If you didn't know him, Old Ned might seem scary. He had thin hair, was balding*, and missing a few teeth. He was wrinkly*, his beard was a mess and he was always dirty. He loved the junk* in his yard. His overalls were stained* with oil and rust* and other types of mud and dirt, but he was a kind person.

Claire tried to picture Old Ned after a good wash, clean-shaven, with teeth. He would look perfectly normal. Who cares whether* he had a family, a wife and children or mother or father?

George's voice echoed in her head. *'He's the keeper of ghosts.'*

Claire shook her head as she ran towards the junkyard gates. Everybody knew there was no such thing as ghosts. Rosie was a chicken for running away. She was going to feel silly at school tomorrow when Claire told everyone about the train. She felt in her pocket for her Dad's mobile phone. This time she'd come prepared. She was going to get a picture of that train and prove* to Rosie and George that there was a steam train in the junkyard.

The gate was still closed. She wondered if she could climb over, and then she noticed that whilst the chain and padlock were wrapped* around the gates, the padlock was open. She was able to push the gates open by just enough so she could wriggle through. Once inside, she pulled them closed again.

As she picked her way across the junkyard, the setting sun lit up the mountains of junk. Claire felt like she had entered another world and a shiver* ran down her spine. She'd only be two minutes. She planned to hold the camera up to the gap in the door and snap a few pictures and then run home.

When she arrived at the big wooden doors, her heart leapt*. The padlock was open, like the one on the front gate.

Claire's heart bounced around inside her chest* as she pulled the door open. There it was. A rusty blue steam engine and a short carriage with the word 'Pullman' spelled out in capital letters across the top.

She gasped, it was more wonderful than she'd thought when she'd first seen it through the gap. Claire walked up to the steam engine, reaching her hands up to touch it. Her fingertips felt the prickle of rust.

'You are beautiful,' she whispered. 'With some paint and a bit of polish* you'd be as good as new.'

She opened the carriage door and stepped up, into the train. Inside, things were in a poor* condition. Most of the windows were cracked*, the wooden floor was covered in dirt and the seats were moulding*, but the place oozed* potential.

'This would be a brilliant hide-out* or club house,' Claire whispered to herself. 'Wait till Rosie sees it.'

A noise startled* her. She spun* around and saw a pale face at the far window of the carriage.

'He's a ghost keeper!' George's voice whispered in her mind. Claire felt a jolt of terror. She shouldn't be here. It was getting dark. She moved backwards slowly, trying not to make a sound. She felt a scream building in her chest. Jumping down from the train, she dashed* through the shed door, and sprinted back through the junkyard. She didn't stop running until she was back home.

4 Bluebell Mystery

George was silent all the way home. Rosie asked him what it was that he'd seen but he shook his head, refusing* to reply.

'Little brothers are weird,' Rosie thought, but she left George alone because he'd been weird ever since Dad had left to go and live in America with a blond woman called Melanie.

An hour later, when Rosie went down to the kitchen for dinner, she found it was only her and her mother eating.

'Isn't George having any dinner?' Rosie asked, as her mother put a bowl of pudding on the table. 'He loves apple pie and custard*.'

'He's at David's house. They're working on a geography project together. He should be back soon. I said I wanted him home before dark. He'll get his apple pie and custard then.'

'He went back out?' Rosie was surprised.

Her mother nodded.

'Mum, what do you know about Old Ned?' Rosie asked, thinking of Claire's steam train and the story George had told about Old Ned being a ghost keeper.

'I know he's not all that old.' Her mother laughed.

'Do you know anything about his family, or what he did before the junkyard?'

Her Mum shook her head. 'It feels like he's always had the junkyard. I remember, when I was a little girl, there was some kind of tragedy* that he was connected with.' She paused to think. 'I'm sorry. I don't know. Why?'

'Oh nothing. George said Old Ned had worked in a funeral parlour and gone to prison.'

'Ha! That's nonsense someone has made* up,' her mother laughed. 'Old Ned wouldn't hurt a fly, and we'd all know if he had been to prison.'

'That's what I thought,' Rosie nodded.

'Why this fascination with Old Ned?'

'Oh, nothing, Claire was at the junkyard today,' Rosie replied. She wondered whether* Claire had seen a steam train in that shed, or if it had been a collection of junk* that just looked like a steam train. It seemed odd* to Rosie that you could put a whole train in a shed. Trains were awfully big. And why would you want to hide something like that?

The more she thought about it, the more questions Rosie had. Why was it that everyone knew Old Ned, but nobody knew anything about him? Rosie took her bowl to the sink*, washed the dishes* and decided to do some research.

Climbing the stairs she went to the spare bedroom. It had once been her father's office. Now it was the computer room and a room for when Granny and Grandpa came to visit.

Turning the machine on, she sat on the wooden stool in front of the screen and typed: old steam train, Barry, Wales, Old Ned. She stopped typing. She didn't even know his real name! Old Ned was very mysterious.

Pictures and stories about steam trains popped up. There were hundreds of them. Rosie was surprised how beautiful steam engines were, but there was nothing about an old train in a shed in a junkyard in Barry, Wales.

Rosie was about to give up scrolling when a blog post caught her eye. It was about a steam train accident in Barry. She clicked on it and read about a terrible rail* accident that had happened forty years ago. Several people had died. There was an old black and white picture. The steam engine had a name. She scribbled it down in her notebook.

She underlined it.

The computer in the school library had an archive of old newspaper stories. Tomorrow, when she got to school, she would go to the library and see if she could find out more about the Bluebell.

5 A Lie

As soon as George got home, he went into the living room. His mum was sitting on the sofa with her feet up, drinking a cup of tea. She worked in the local supermarket. Since Dad had left and gone to America, she'd had to work longer hours.

'George, sit down and have a cup of tea with me.' She smiled at him. She looked tired.

'I can't, Mum. I've got some really important homework to do,' George said, sitting down next to her on the sofa. 'It's a big geography project for Mr Barking,' he lied.

'Well, off you go then and get it done.' She took a big gulp from her mug of tea.

'I'm doing the project with David. I was wondering if I could go to his house to do it.'

'When?'

'Now.'

'But I've got us lamb* chops for dinner.'

'I'll have them when I get back.' George clasped his hands together and made a pleading* face.

'Alright,' his mum smiled, '... and the apple pie and custard*?'

'Save that too.' George kissed his mum's cheek*. Apple pie and custard was his favourite pudding.

She smiled and ruffled his hair 'It's nice to see you enthusiastic about geography. Off you go to David's. I don't mind.'

'Thanks Mum', he said, spinning* around and running upstairs to his bedroom.

He emptied his rucksack of school books. Pulling a shoe box out from under his bed, he opened it and put the contents* into his bag:

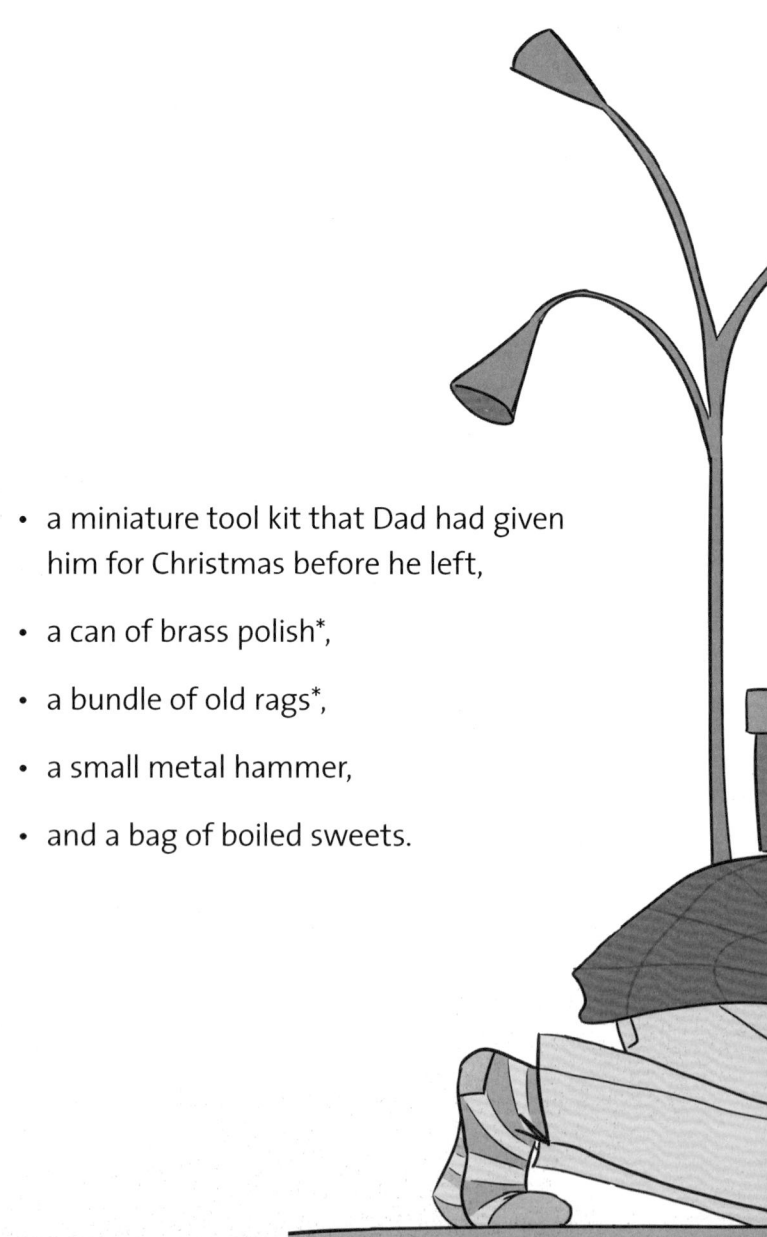

- a miniature tool kit that Dad had given him for Christmas before he left,

- a can of brass polish*,

- a bundle of old rags*,

- a small metal hammer,

- and a bag of boiled sweets.

Opening the top drawer* of the desk in his bedroom, George pulled out a notebook held together with an elastic band. It was stuffed with bits of paper. He slipped* it into the front pocket of his bag. He grabbed the torch from his desk, put it into the pocket of his coat and pulled on a woolly hat. He was ready.

Listening at the door, he heard Rosie talking to
Mum. He listened as she climbed the stairs and
went into her bedroom. He heard the door close.
Very quietly, George slipped* out of his bedroom
and went down the stairs, missing out the fourth
step because it creaked*.

'Bye, Mum, see you later,' George said in a low voice, before creeping out into the front garden. He had to be quick. If Rosie looked out the window, she would see him. He dashed* along the path, out onto the pavement and ducked down behind the wall. He crouched, as he scurried* along the road, only standing up straight once he was far enough away for Rosie not to see him.

Looking over his shoulder, to make sure that he wasn't being followed, George went back to the junkyard.

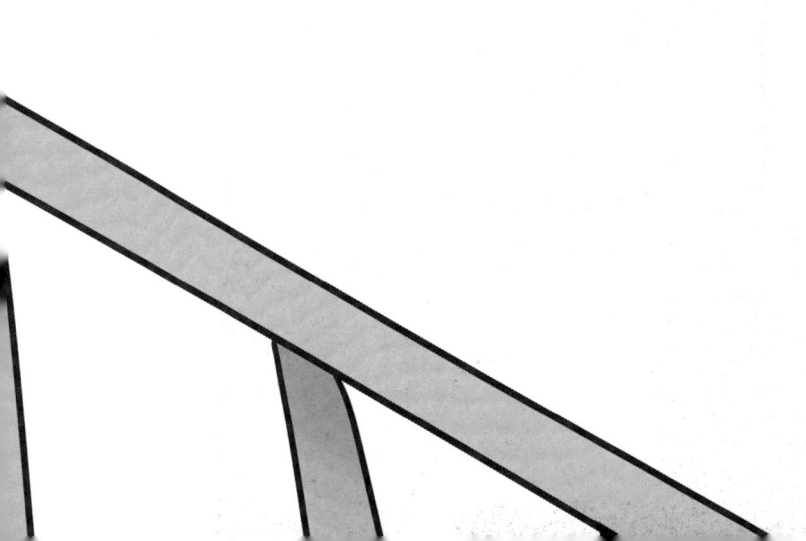

6 Bad Dreams

Claire didn't sleep well. She woke up twice in the night, startled by the sight of a pale face in her dreams. In her dreams, she was chased* round and round the old junkyard by a wailing* ghost. Each time she thought she had found an escape, Old Ned was standing in the way, wearing his dirty baseball cap and holding a spanner*.

Claire shuddered* and looked out the window, happy to see the sun. She got dressed in her black and purple school uniform, ate her breakfast and grabbed her bag. She walked round to Rosie and George's house, like she did every day. Usually they were waiting outside for her, but not today. She knocked on the door of Number 53, but nobody answered.

'That's odd*,' thought Claire and when she looked up at the windows, they were dark. She tried again. No answer. 'They've gone to school without me!' Claire looked at her watch. She wasn't even late. She knocked on the door really loudly, one last time, to make sure there was nobody at home, then angrily stomped back down the garden path to walk to school on her own. 'How mean*,' she thought, 'especially after I took them to see the steam train.'

'Hey Claire, what's up?'

Three of her classmates were standing by the pelican* crossing.

'Hi Janet, hi Simon, hi Margaret.' Claire crossed the road, falling into step beside them.

'Where's Rosie?' Margaret asked.

'She's gone on without me,' Claire whispered angrily.

'Did you two have a fight?' Janet asked.

Claire shrugged.

'Then what's her problem?' Janet said.

'I don't know.' Claire shook her head. 'I think I might have freaked* her out yesterday.'

'Freaked her out? How?' Simon asked.

'I was poking around in Old Ned's junkyard, getting bits for my robot project, when I found a locked up old shed and you'll never guess what I saw inside?'

'What?' Simon and Margaret leaned towards her.

'An old steam train,' Claire said, watching their faces for their reaction.

'No way,' Simon said, obviously* impressed.

'That's awesome!' Margaret said.

'It is, isn't it?' Claire said, pleased* that finally someone was reacting in the way that she thought they should.

'Most trains are boring, but old steam engines are cool I guess,' Janet said. 'But, why would you discovering a train freak out Rosie?'

'I took Rosie and George to the junkyard last night to show it to them. We couldn't get in because the gate was locked. George was nervous because he'd heard this story about the junkyard being haunted, and it was getting dark, and then... we saw a ghost!

'No way,' Janet said. 'Are you being serious?'

'I don't like ghosts,' Margaret said.

'Ghosts aren't real,' Simon laughed.

'They are,' Claire nodded. 'I went back, on my own, later and I saw it with my own eyes. I'm telling you – there's a steam train in Old Ned's junkyard, and it is haunted.'

'Brilliant,' Simon said. 'When can we see it?'

'I've got an idea,' Claire said. 'Let's have a ghost hunt*.'

'A ghost hunt?' Margaret squeaked*.

'On Saturday,' Claire nodded, 'as it's getting dark. We'll go to the junkyard. I'll show you the train and we can hunt for ghosts. George says he's heard a story about Old Ned working in a funeral parlour and now he's a ghost keeper.'

'Maybe the ghosts want to be set free?' Margaret said. 'Maybe he's trapping* them?'

'Maybe,' Janet said, looking unconvinced.

'Ned isn't a ghost keeper,' Simon laughed. 'There's no such thing as ghosts.'

'Let's find out, shall we?' Claire said. 'Who's up for a ghost hunt on Saturday?'

'I'm in,' Simon agreed. 'I want to see the train.'

'Alright,' Margaret whimpered.
Janet shrugged. 'I haven't got anything better to do.'

7 Edward Woodham

Rosie had set her alarm for half an hour earlier than usual. She washed her face, pulled on her school uniform and grabbed her rucksack.

Running down the stairs, she grabbed an apple for breakfast and took a bite as she slipped* out the front door, closing it behind her.

She thought for a moment about Claire. They always walked to school together. She shrugged; George would tell her Rosie had gone early. She'd explain to Claire why when she saw her later.

Rosie wanted to get to school early, so that she could get on the library computer and search for stories about the Bluebell steam engine. Claire would be pleased* to learn the train she'd seen in Old Ned's shed was real and had a dramatic story behind it.

Excited, Rosie half walked, half ran to school. She felt like a detective with a lead* on a case. When she arrived at school, the gates were open, but the playground was empty. She went into the main building to the library. The door was shut. She knocked gently* and peered through the thick glass. After a few minutes, she saw Mrs Bibble coming. There was a click and the door opened.

'Yes dear?' Mrs Bibble blinked at her through thick round glasses.

'Good morning Mrs Bibble. I was wondering if I could use the library computer? I've got some homework to finish before school starts.'

'Of course.' Mrs Bibble opened the door wide. 'You're more than welcome, Rosie. I was just pouring myself a mug of tea.'

'You finish your tea,' Rosie said. 'I know how to turn the computer on.'

'Thank you, Rosie,' Mrs Bibble smiled and blinked. 'I'll be here behind the desk if you need me'.

Rosie put her bag on the floor and sat down in front of a computer. She pressed the button to turn it on, pulling out her notebook and pen. Rosie clicked on the News Archive icon, which linked to the national newspaper archives. She'd used it before for a history project on the Queen's Gold Jubilee. She typed *Bluebell, steam train, accident, Barry, Wales* into the search box. A list of stories came back. She double clicked on the first one.

The front page of the *The Daily Post* filled the screen. The headline said:

Five Killed in Bluebell Rail Tragedy

The picture was shocking, even in black and white. The heavy engine was on its side, a part of its metal panelling* ripped* open. Looking inside the engine was like looking inside a human being. Rosie could see small and large tubes*, like metal veins* and intestines. She read the article.

Five Killed in Bluebell Rail Tragedy

On Wednesday, 27 August 1961 at 9.23 a.m. the Bluebell – a Hall Class locomotive pulling a carriage of passengers – collided* with an empty coal truck which had fallen onto the rails.

The train had been travelling at 27 miles an hour and the collision derailed* the engine and the carriage, causing an explosion in the firebox. This tragic accident resulted in five deaths, including the driver and the fireman, and seven seriously injured* passengers. Tragically, Mr and Mrs Woodham and

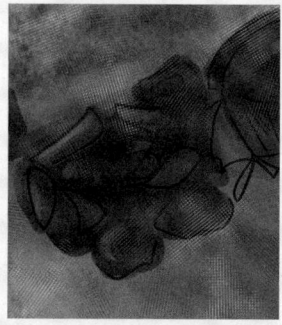

their seven-year-old son Bertrand were among the passengers killed in the accident, leaving a young boy, two-year-old Edward Woodham, an orphan*.

R

'Edward Woodham! People often shorten the name Edward to Ned.' Rosie looked at the date. 'If Edward Woodham is Old Ned, that would make Ned over sixty.' She thought of Old Ned in his baseball cap, and dirty overalls with his bushy beard. This seemed about the right age.

Reading the rest of the article, Rosie learned that the railway line, which had only been used by local people going to Cardiff, was losing money and had been closed after the accident. With a bit more exploring, she discovered the line had never reopened.

Rosie wrote down the details of the accident in her notebook and copied the paragraph about Edward Woodham word for word.

'Poor Old Ned,' thought Rosie. He was orphaned* by the train he keeps hidden in the junkyard. She thought about the ghost George had seen. 'Maybe the ghosts are Ned's family? Maybe the ghost keeper takes care of the train, because it's haunted by the ghosts of his mother, father and brother Bertrand. A shiver* ran down Rosie's spine. She felt that she was on to something.

8 George's Secret

George spent his day keeping out of the way of Rosie or Claire. Whenever he saw them in the corridor on their way to lessons, he would duck into a doorway. He didn't want to talk to them about the steam train in the junkyard.

As soon as the bell rang at the end of the day, he dashed out of the school gates, running to the junkyard to find Old Ned.

'Hello,' he called, 'anybody here?' He heard barking, and Bodger, Old Ned's giant bull mastiff* ran to him, jumping up and licking* his face. 'Hello boy, how are you?' George gave the dog a big cuddle*.

'Welcome, young George,' Old Ned came out of his cabin, smiling.

The cabin may have once stood alone, but over the years countless items* had been piled* up around it, so that it looked like a door and a window in a hillside of rusting metal and old furniture.

Old Ned wiped* his hands on his overalls and shook George by the hand. 'How about doing some fixing* today?'

'I came to see you yesterday evening,' George said. 'The place was open, but I couldn't find you.'

'Must've forgotten to put the padlock on.' Old Ned shrugged. 'I was out collecting a couple of burnt out cars from Lavernock. I had to take the tow* truck.'

'Something terrible has happened,' George said in his most serious voice.

'What's that?' Old Ned said.

'Claire, my sister's best friend, has discovered the Bluebell.'

'Has she now?"

'She came in yesterday looking for parts for her robot project, went around the back to the old shed and peered in. She saw the train'. George bit his lip. 'What are we going to do?'

'There's not much we can do. She can have a look if she wants.'

'Yes, but then she tried to bring me and Rosie back to see it.'

'Oh dear.'

'I scared Claire and Rosie off. I told them the junkyard was haunted.'

Old Ned laughed. 'Did you now?'

'Yes, but what if they come back? The Bluebell is our secret.'

'We'll worry when it happens. We've got work to do this afternoon.'

'What if someone sees us?' George looked over his shoulder.

Old Ned marched to the gate, wrapped* the chain around it and locked the padlock, turning a sign over. 'See,' he pointed. 'Closed'.

George grinned, and patted* his rucksack. 'I've brought my tools, and the polish.'

'I've found a pressure* gauge for us to fit today.'

'I'll scrub the rust off the levers* in the cabin with the wire* brush and give them a polish.'

'If we put some oil on them, we may get them to move again,' Old Ned said, as they made their way through the junkyard to the steam engine shed.

George had first come to the junkyard when his dad had left. Old Ned had been kind and let him explore. George loved to take engines apart* and put them back together again. He had his own tool kit. One day, Old Ned had done something he thought he would never do: He had taken George to the hidden shed round the back of the junkyard, taken the padlock off the door, and shown him the Bluebell.

George had fallen in love with the steam engine right there and then. Old Ned suggested that they should try and fix the rusty old engine together. He had collected spare* parts over the years and there were a lot of useful bits and pieces in the junkyard. They had been working on the engine for a year now.

George was happiest when he was with Old Ned, working on the steam train.

Old Ned climbed up into the cab* of the Bluebell, and then helped George up. George pulled out the polish, picked up the wire brush and worked away at levers whilst Old Ned put in the pressure gauge.

The pair worked away happily in silence, safe in the knowledge that the gate was locked and that they wouldn't be disturbed*.

9 Fallout

Rosie was angry. Claire had avoided* her all day
yesterday and today she hadn't turned up to walk
to school. Rosie had waited for her and now she
was late.

'Hey, Rosie,' Janet called to her as she hurried into
school. 'Have you heard? Claire's discovered a
haunted train in the junkyard. Tomorrow night,
we're going to have a ghost hunt*.
Are you coming?'

'A ghost hunt?' Rosie frowned.

'Yeah, a ghost hunt,' Claire said coming to stand beside Janet. Margaret and Simon were right behind her.

'Where were you this morning?' Rosie asked.
'I waited.'

'Where were you yesterday?' Claire asked.
'I waited.'

'Are you coming to hunt for ghosts?' Janet asked Rosie.

'You can come if you want,' Claire said.

'We're meeting at the park at the end of my road and then I'm leading the ghost hunters to the junkyard.'

'Do you think that's a good idea?' Rosie said, trying to signal to Claire with her eyes that it wasn't.

'Yes. I think it's a great idea,' Claire said. 'Why are you looking at me like that?'

'I think we should stay away from the junkyard,' Rosie said.

Simon made the noise of a wailing* ghost. 'Are you scared?'

Claire crossed her arms and frowned. 'Ever since I discovered the steam engine, you've been mean* to me. You wish you'd found it first, don't you? You're jealous.'

Janet and Margaret crossed their arms, too, and moved closer to Claire. 'Well you didn't discover

it, I did,' Claire said, 'and we are going to have a ghost hunt on Saturday whether* you like it or not.'

'Ghost hunt?' George came running up the corridor. 'What ghost hunt?'

'You'll never guess what's happened.' Simon stepped towards George. 'Claire has discovered a steam train in Old Ned's junkyard, but it's haunted, which is even more brilliant!' He waved his hands with excitement. 'Tomorrow night, Claire's leading a ghost hunt. We're going to find the train and try and see some ghosts. You can come if you want. Everyone's going to be there.'

'George is scared of ghosts,' Rosie said.

'No, I'm not!' George replied.

'Why did you scream and run away the other day then?' Rosie asked.

'If you're scared, perhaps you should stay at home,' Simon said.

'I don't want to come, but not because I'm scared,' George replied. 'I've played all over that junkyard. If there was a train there, I'd have seen it. You're wasting your time.'

'No we're not.' Claire's face went purple as she glared at him.

'There is a train in that junkyard. I saw it.'

'I think what you saw were mountains of junk which looked like a train. You didn't get a clear look.' Claire scowled as George was talking. 'I'm not spending my Saturday night walking all the way to the junkyard, in the dark and cold, to pick my way through mouldy* rubbish finding nothing, when there's such good TV programmes on in my nice warm house.'

Claire looked like steam was about to come out of her ears, she was so angry.

'Well, we ARE going, and now neither of you are invited,' Claire snapped.

'Fine by me,' George said, 'but you're going to look stupid when you don't find a train, or any ghosts.'

Janet and Margaret looked up at Claire.

'There is a train there,' Claire shouted, 'and there are ghosts!'

10 Halt the Hunt

Claire stomped away into the school building.

'Claire, wait!' Rosie called, running after her.

Claire looked back over her shoulder, whilst Janet and Margaret hurried to her side.

'I need to talk to you,' Rosie said.

Claire narrowed her eyes. 'Well I don't want to talk to you.'

'Please, Claire. There's something I need to tell you.'

Claire looked suspicious*. 'Go on then. I'm listening.'

'Alone,' Rosie looked at Margaret and Janet.

'Anything you need to tell me, you can tell me in front of my friends.' Rosie noticed how Claire emphasised* the word friends.

'You mustn't go to Old Ned's junkyard. It's a bad idea.'

'Why?' Claire said. 'Why don't you simply tell us what the problem is?'

'I... I can't.' Rosie looked at the floor.

Claire laughed. 'Thought not. You've got nothing to say.'

'I don't want to say it in front of everybody.' Rosie said quietly, pleading* with her eyes.

'Are we not good enough for you?' Janet asked. 'Is that it?'

'No. It's not that,' Rosie stammered*. 'It's a private matter*.'

George had followed his sister, and he could see that she was getting upset*.

'Well I don't want to listen,' Claire replied. 'I am going to the junkyard tomorrow to see that train and hunt ghosts, and you can't stop me.'

'Yeah,' said Simon.

'And you're not welcome,' Margaret added.

'Don't wait for me in the mornings anymore,' Claire said. 'I'm walking to school with Janet and Margaret now.'

'Claire!' Rosie's hands flew to her face.

Janet and Margaret linked arms with Claire and the three of them walked away down the corridor laughing.

'Oh!' Rosie's cheeks* were flushed pink.

George thought she might be about to cry. 'With friends like that, who needs enemies, eh?' He said, giving his sister's arm a gentle* pat*.

'Shut up!' Rosie shouted at him. 'You just shut up. Claire is my oldest and best friend. She's the only person I can talk to about Dad being gone, and now, because of her stupid train, I have no one.' A tear rolled down her cheek. 'I wish I'd never heard anything about her train.'

'It is not her train,' George said. 'Why do people keep saying it's her train?'

Rosie glared at him. 'I thought you didn't even believe there was a train?'

'I... I don't,' George stammered. 'I was saying that, just because you see a train, doesn't mean it belongs to you. She only thinks she saw a train. We don't know that what she saw was a real train. It could have been anything, so how can the train be hers...?'

'Stop talking. I don't want to listen.' Rosie wiped* her eyes with her sleeve. 'I believe Claire saw a train, a real steam train,' she sniffed*, 'but I also know that leading half the class down to the junkyard to hunt for railway* ghosts would be a terrible thing to do.' She walked away from her brother George, shaking her head. 'Somehow, I have to stop her.'

11 The Mission

'So, what's the plan for tomorrow, Claire?' Margaret asked as they sat down in the dining hall with their lunch trays*.

They could all see that Claire was still angry about her argument with Rosie.

'You're not going to listen to Rosie are you?' Janet scoffed.

'Are you getting cold feet?' Simon said.

'No,' Claire replied, 'No, I'm not. And I'm not going to change my mind, no matter* what Rosie says. We are going to the junkyard tomorrow night to see that train.'

Janet smiled. 'Great, so what's the plan?'

'We can't meet at my house. Mum and Dad will get suspicious,' Claire explained. 'Let's meet at the park at the bottom of my road at six o'clock. I'll tell my Mum that I'm coming to yours, Janet, to watch a film.

'Cool,' Janet nodded.

'Once we've met up, we'll all head to Old Ned's junkyard together and I'll show you where the train is'.

'Should we wear anything special?' Margaret said. 'I've never hunted ghosts before.'

'It will be cold,' Claire said. 'We should wrap* up warm.'

'Everyone should wear dark colours, like navy blue and black, so that we can hide easily,' Simon said.

'We'll need torches,' Janet added.

'Yes, and some of us should bring cameras so we can take pictures,' Claire nodded. 'We need evidence*, so we can prove that the train exists.'

'What about Old Ned?' Margaret asked.

'What about him?' Claire said.

'Well, do you think he'll be there?' Margaret said.

'I don't know,' Claire frowned.

'I thought he lived there,' Janet said, 'with that big dog.'

'Why would anyone want to live in a junkyard?' Margaret said.

'I don't think he has a choice,' Simon said. 'We don't need to worry about the dog. He's big but friendly and doesn't bite.'

'But he might* give us away,' Claire said. 'What if he barks?'

'I'll bring a bag of dog treats*,' Margaret said. 'My aunt has a dog, and he'll do anything for dog treats, even tricks. If Old Ned's dog barks, then we'll give him some treats to keep him quiet.'

'What about Old Ned? What if he's there?' Janet asked. 'What do we do?'

'Well, if he is there and he sees us, then we'll ask to see the train,' Claire replied, boldly*. 'We're not doing anything wrong.'

'What if he won't let us?' Janet said.

'What if he sets his ghosts on us?' Margaret asked.

'Then we'll rush* him, get our cameras out and capture* the evidence,' Claire said. 'If Old Ned is a ghost keeper, then we'll tell the newspapers and show them the pictures.'

'We'll be heroes,' Simon said, his mouth full of food.

'This is going to be fun,' Janet grinned.

'You wait till you see this train. It's beautiful, and there's a carriage with tables and chandeliers*,' Claire smiled. 'It will make a brilliant club house.'

'Six o'clock in the park,' Simon said.

Claire nodded. 'Tomorrow at six we'll catch a train and hunt for ghosts.'

12 The Grandfather Clock Plan

On the way home from school, Rosie's heart felt heavy. She was walking alone. Her friendship with Claire was in jeopardy*. She couldn't understand why they had argued over a train. Rosie wanted to talk to Claire, but her old friend was so angry with her it seemed impossible.

'If I could only explain that I do believe there's a train in that shed,' Rosie whispered to herself, 'and that I'm not jealous.' She shook her head. It would be terrible for Claire, if she brought everyone to the junkyard. Ned kept his secrets for a reason. He might become very angry with her and not let the children use the junkyard anymore. He might tell their parents. Claire could be in big trouble.

Rosie thought about Old Ned, building his life and his work around that train, of the junk that he had piled* up on top of the painful* memory. He had literally* buried* it. She wondered if the train was his link to his mum, dad and brother.

Rosie missed her dad terribly, even though she was angry with him for leaving. She felt she understood why Old Ned might keep the train a secret, away from prying* eyes.

What Claire was planning to do was wrong and would upset Old Ned. Claire would feel terrible in the end and might get into trouble. Somehow, Rosie had to stop the ghost hunt.

When Rosie got home, she went straight up to her bedroom and lay on her bed, thinking.

'I need to find a way to help Old Ned that won't upset Claire.' She put her hands behind her head and stared at the ceiling*, thinking about the ghost hunt plan, and then she had an idea. 'I'll go to the junkyard before Claire gets there with everyone,' she thought. 'I'll find some really good junk for Old Ned to collect and take him out of the yard. That way, he won't be in the yard when Claire and the others are hunting for the ghosts. They'll discover the train but when there are no ghosts, they'll soon get bored and leave.'

Rosie felt a thrill of excitement in her stomach. 'When Old Ned comes back, he'll never know they were there. No one will get hurt.' She felt pleased. 'All I need to do now is find a great bit of junk that Old Ned won't be able to resist*.'

After some thinking, Rosie sat up. She remembered that Mrs Harkett, from down the road, had put a beautiful grandfather clock in her front garden. It was covered with an old blanket*. Rosie had asked what it was, and Mrs Harkett had told her that she'd always hated the clock because it had very loud chimes*. It had been in her husband's family for years. When her husband had died, Mrs Harkett felt as though the clock was chiming her doom* and so had dragged* it out of the house. Rosie wondered if the old clock was still there. She knew Old Ned liked clocks. The one time she'd been in his cabin she'd seen lots of pocket watches and clocks being taken apart* on his workbench. She decided that tomorrow morning she would knock on Mrs Harkett's door and offer to bring Old Ned over to take the clock away that very evening.

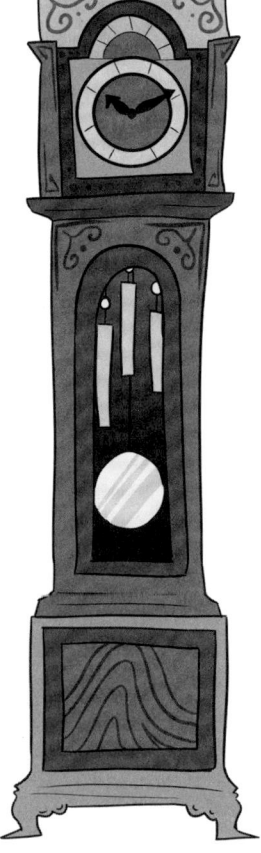

Everything felt like it was coming together. It occurred* to Rosie that once Claire had her photographic evidence*, Old Ned might not be able to keep the Bluebell a secret for much longer. However, she was sure that if Claire knew that Old Ned was poor little Edward Woodham, she'd want to keep his train a secret too. After the silly ghost hunt was over, Rosie would tell Claire Old Ned's story.

13 Train Haunting

The bell rang. It was the end of school. George stuffed his books into his rucksack and hurried to the gates. He ran all the way to the junkyard.

'Ned,' he called, 'Ned, it's George, where are you?' George stopped to give Bodger a pat. 'Where is he boy? Where's Old Ned?'

George heard a clank followed by a couple of twangs. Ned was working in the yard. Following the sound of metal hitting metal, George found Ned with his head in the bonnet of a car. He had a spanner* in his hand.

'Ned!' George called, hurrying over. Old Ned looked up. He had engine grease* all over his hands.

'I need to talk to you. It's important.' George spoke fast. 'There's going to be a ghost hunt on Saturday and...'

'A ghost hunt?' Old Ned smiled. 'Now why would you want to go hunting for things that don't exist?'

'Not me. It's these kids at school, and, oh Ned, it's awful. They are coming here to hunt for ghosts and it's my fault*.'

'Slow down.' Old Ned wiped his hands on a cloth*. 'Start from the beginning.'

'Claire, my sister's friend, the one who came here to look for robot parts and saw the train ... Well she believes what I told her, about the yard being haunted.'

Old Ned laughed.

'It's not funny,' George said. 'She's told all the kids in school that you're a ghost keeper, and that there's an old haunted train in the shed, and now they're all going to come here on Saturday evening to see the steam train in your shed and catch ghosts'.

'They might be a bit disappointed,' said Old Ned with a smile. 'I've never seen any ghosts near that train, nor anywhere around the yard'.

'This is serious,' George said, frustrated that Ned didn't seem as upset as he felt. 'How are we going to stop them?'

'Maybe we shouldn't stop them,' Old Ned said. 'It's not right to keep that beautiful old thing all to ourselves, George. The Bluebell was made to carry many people. Maybe it's about time that we showed the world all the hard work that we've been doing.'

'But I don't want to share the Bluebell. It's our train, it's our secret.'

'Secrets aren't good George. Secrets can cause* trouble. Look at what happened when you tried to keep the train secret from your sister's friend.'

'I don't want everyone knowing about our train. If everybody knows it's here, they'll all want to play with it. It's... it's special.'
'I see.' Old Ned's brown eyes looked down at George. 'Well, perhaps we can find a way to enjoy the discovery of the train.'

'I doubt* it,' George sulked*.

'What do you say about us joining in with this ghost hunt...?'

'Joining in?'

'Well, if they're going to come looking for ghosts, maybe we should give them some!' Old Ned's eyes sparkled.

'You mean, scare them?' George's face lit up.

'Give them a train haunting they'll never forget,' Old Ned grinned. 'They might get so scared they never want to come back. What do you say?'

'I say that is a brilliant idea,' George grinned.

14 The Ghost Hunt

Rosie wrote a note to her mum, saying she was going over to Claire's house and left it on the kitchen table. Pulling on her coat, Rosie checked the time. It was five thirty. She had to get to the junkyard before Claire and the others did.

Rosie walked quickly through the cold autumnal evening. When she arrived at the junkyard, the gate was open and the chain with the padlock was on the ground.

'Hello,' she called, 'anybody there?'

Bodger galloped towards her. 'Hello boy.' She patted his head and scratched behind his ears.

'I'm looking for Ned. Do you know where he is?' She went to Ned's cabin, but there was no sign of him. Hanging outside the cabin was an old bell with a rope, a large knot* tied in the end. Rosie gave the bell a ring and waited. Sure enough, a few minutes later Old Ned appeared*.

'Hello young lady, how may I help you?' he asked.

'Hello,' Rosie smiled sweetly, 'I've come on an important mission. Do you know Mrs Harkett who lives on my road? Well her husband died.'

'I'm sorry to hear that.' Old Ned bowed his head.

'That's why I need your help. You see, she has this beautiful old grandfather clock that used to belong to him, and every time it chimes* it upsets her. It's so bad that she's dragged* it out of the house and into her front garden. That's how I know about it. It's a wonderful old clock, seven foot tall and the clock and everything inside works really well. But that doesn't matter, because it makes Mrs Harkett cry. I told her that you might take it away and she was so delighted that she said you could have it for free if you took it right this very minute.

'Well, I'm afraid I'm a little busy right now,' Old Ned said.

'Oh, doing what?' Rosie looked around. 'Can't it wait?'

Old Ned shuffled from one foot to another. 'Nothing much I suppose.'

'The clock really is beautiful. It's probably worth a lot of money.' Rosie crossed her fingers behind her back and smiled. 'It'll only take ten minutes.'

'Alright,' Old Ned looked over his shoulder. 'Wait here a second.'

Rosie played with Bodger's ears while she waited. Old Ned was back a few minutes later. 'Let's go and take a look at this clock,' he said, pulling on his baseball cap.

'Brilliant.' Rosie smiled.

As they were leaving the yard, Rosie stumbled*.

'Ouch, oh I think I've twisted my ankle*.' She looked at Ned. 'We're going to have to walk slowly.'

'Here, let me help you.' Old Ned looked back over his shoulder again. 'I can't leave the yard for too long.'

Five minutes after Rosie had led Old Ned off down the road, Claire and the ghost hunters arrived. There were nine of them, dressed in black and navy blue, their heads wrapped* up with bobble hats and scarves. They crept along the pavement towards the junkyard.

'This is it,' Claire said, delighted to see the junkyard gates were open. 'Are we all together?'

They grabbed at one another, giggling excitedly. Lots of heads nodded. 'Yes, yes, yes,' came the replies.

'And you've got your cameras and torches?'

'Yes, yes, yes!' the whispers came again.

'Ok,' Claire said. 'Follow me'.

Claire entered the junkyard first. Bodger bounded over and licked her. 'Good dog,' she said. 'Sit!' Bodger sat. Claire crept towards the cabin, Bodger followed her, wagging his tail*. 'Who's got the dog treats*?' she hissed*.

'I do. Here Bodger,' Margaret came forward and put down a trail* of dog treats leading towards the gates. The happy dog crunched them up as the children scurried* past.

Claire climbed over the bonnet of a yellow car, to a thin winding path into the mountains of metal and wood. 'This way.' She waved for the others to follow her as she made her way to a clearing* in front of a pair of barn* doors.

'That's funny,' Claire said. 'I'm sure there was more stuff in front of the doors before.'

'Come on,' Janet said, as she and the others ran to the doors.

'The padlock's gone!' Claire said. 'When I've been here before, there's always been a padlock on this door. I wonder where it is.' She pushed the door. It made a creaking* sound and opened just a crack*.

Janet and Margaret looked at each other. Their eyes were wide. A thrill of fear, like electricity, crackled* through the group of children.

'It's dark inside,' Claire said, pushing the door harder. It suddenly swung wide open, making a terrible noise. A couple of the others gasped and slowly moved backwards.

'It's just a creaky door!' Claire said boldly*, stepping into the shed.

Something flew at her face and she screamed, ducking as an owl*, or a bat* maybe, flew over her head.

'What was that?' Janet said.

'A ghost?' Margaret asked.

'No, no. I think it was a bird,' Claire said, a bit shaken. She noticed two of the children at the back of the group turn around and leave. The rest were huddled together. She needed to show them she wasn't afraid. 'Look,' she said, pointing.

'The train!' Simon gasped.

The children ran forwards towards the old steam train.

'It's amazing!' Margaret cried as they all pushed their noses up against the windows and peered into the Pullman carriage.

The lights inside flickered* on and off, then died. All seven of the children gasped and leapt backwards.

'What was THAT?' Claire said. 'It's never done THAT before!'

Margaret looked at Janet. 'I don't like it,' she whispered.

'It was a ghost!' Janet said, thrilled.

Claire didn't want the others to think she was scared. 'I'm going inside,' she said, and climbed the steps of the carriage, opening the door and stepping inside. The lights flickered on and off and on and off again. She panicked, leaping back out of the carriage.

A girl called Gracie, who had had enough, turned and ran out of the barn*.

'Who's doing that?' Claire shouted, looking around.

'It's a ghost,' Janet said.

'Brilliant,' Simon said, sounding frightened.

'Who's got a camera?' Claire asked.

'Err, I do.' A boy called Mark stepped forward.

'We came on a ghost hunt, didn't we?' Claire asked. Five frightened faces nodded back at her. 'So, let's find that ghost. Mark, you take pictures. I'm going back inside.' Taking a deep breath, Claire went back into the carriage. No lights flickered this time. Getting bolder, she pushed her way through a thick mass of cobwebs* she didn't remember seeing last time she was in here.

She stood in the middle of the carriage and held up her hands as if to say, *'there's nothing here'*. The lights started flickering again. She looked up at the chandeliers* and then back at her friends crossing her arms to show that she wasn't scared of the lights.

Her classmates all had looks of horror on their faces. Simon was pointing at something over Claire's shoulder. There was a deafening* hiss as steam exploded out from underneath the train, enveloping* the screaming group of children.

Claire screamed and jumped from the carriage, frightened of what might be behind her. She fell to her knees and saw rails underneath the train. This shed was built on top of railway tracks.

As the steam cleared, Claire saw that only Simon and Janet were left. The others had all run away.

'Quick,' she cried. 'To the engine.'

The three of them peered into the engine cab*, but there was no one there. The furnace* came to life and flames licked the metal doorway.

'Argh!' Simon jumped back, looked at Claire, mouthing the word 'sorry' and ran.

There was another great hiss and suddenly there was steam everywhere.

'Wait for me!' Janet wailed, running after Simon.

'I'm not scared,' Claire told herself as she grabbed the handle* to pull herself up into the cab, and then the train sounded an eerie* whistle. She let go of the handle and screamed as she fell to the ground.

15 Runaway Train

Lying on the ground, Claire looked up past the huge wheels to the cab* of the old rusty engine. Her blood froze* when she saw a pale face at the controls of the train. It was the ghost!

'Help!' she squeaked*, but all her classmates had run away. She was alone.

The ghost turned to face her. Its mouth was open wide. Claire knew she should get up and run but was frozen with terror. And then, she recognised* the ghost.

'George?' She got up on her knees.

He was shouting something, but she couldn't hear him over the noise of steam escaping. There was a loud creaking sound and the engine rolled forward an inch.

'I can't move the lever*!' George shouted. 'I pulled it down, but I can't push it back up! Help me!'

Claire heard the panic in George's voice.

The train creaked forward another inch.

'I don't know which one is for the brakes*!' he cried.

As Claire jumped to her feet, she saw Old Ned and Rosie running into the shed.

'Help,' Claire waved at them. 'George has turned the steam on.'

Old Ned sprinted passed her, leaping up into the cabin, just as the train moved forward. His head hit the metal cab wall and he fell to the ground.

'Ned!' George cried out, dropping to the floor beside him. 'Help me! He's bleeding*!'

Time had made the steam train's wheels stiff and the coupling* rods were rusty, but the power of steam was forcing* the train to creep forwards. Claire cried out, pointing to the front of the train. There was a splintering sound and then a terrible roar as the train pushed through the back wall of the shed and part of the roof came down.

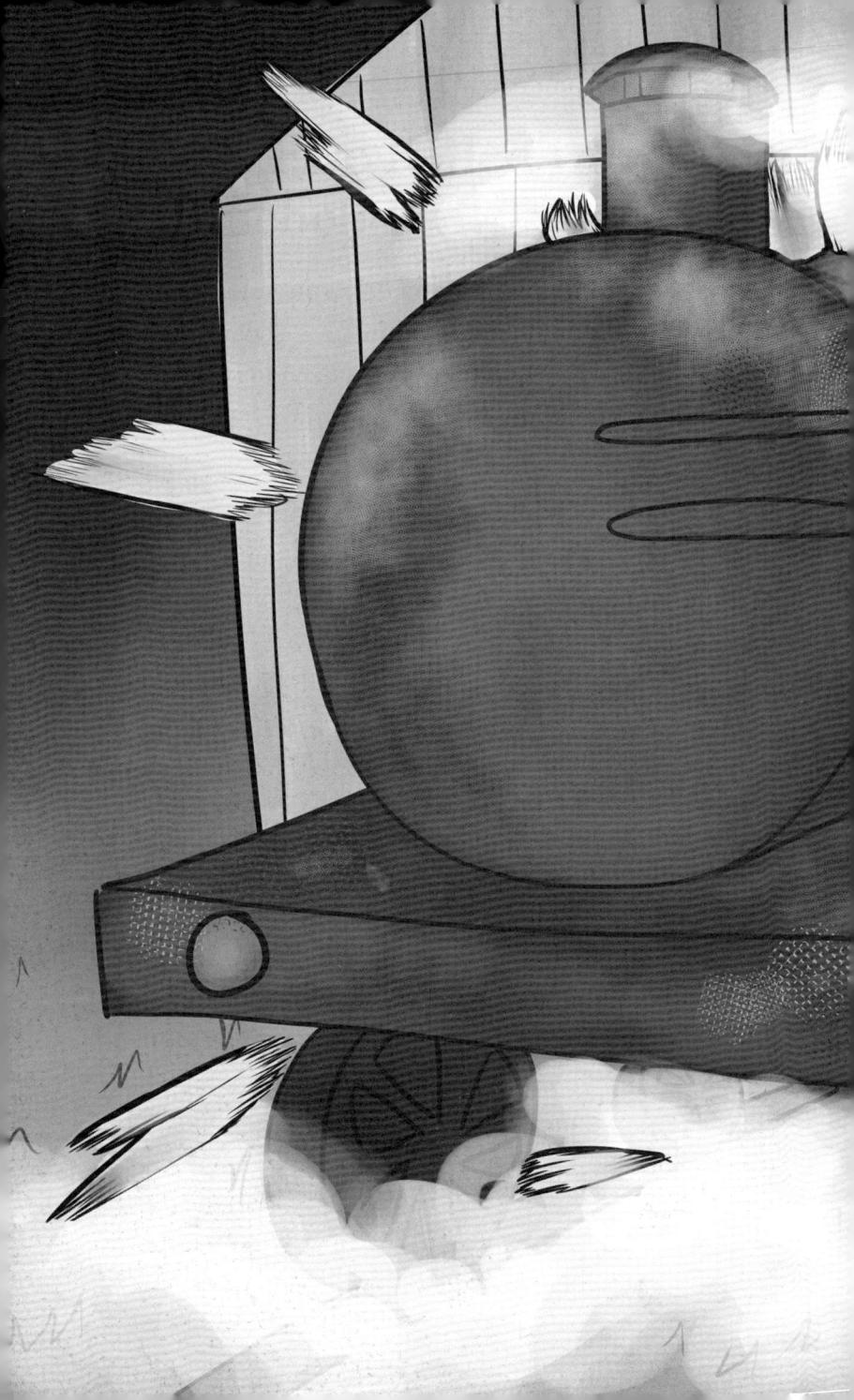

Rosie and Claire ran backward to avoid the falling debris*, but then Rosie was sprinting forwards. She grabbed onto the metal handle on the side of the cab and jumped up onto the footplate.

'George, which lever did you pull down to let the steam out?' she shouted.

George sat on the floor beside Old Ned, his arms wrapped around his knees.

'George! WHICH LEVER?' Rosie screamed.

He pointed up at a lever. Grabbing it with both hands and using all of her strength*, Rosie pushed and pushed until the lever had gone from south to north, but the train was still rolling.

'We need to put out the fire!' George said.

Rosie grabbed the fire bucket which was full of sand and threw it into the furnace, putting out the flames. A cloud of smoke pushed her backwards. She dropped down beside George and gently shook Old Ned's shoulder.

'He's dead,' George said, staring at the blood trickling down his head. 'It's all my fault*.'

'He's not dead,' Rosie said. 'Look, he's breathing. Ned, wake up, please wake up. I need to know which lever is the brake.' The train was slowing down, but it was still moving and there were terrible noises as it crushed bicycles and other bits of metal between the rails and its huge wheels.

'Ned, please,' Rosie shook him harder.

Old Ned blinked. He raised his hand and pointed his finger at a small lever on the side of the cab. Rosie spun* around and yanked* it down. There was a squealing sound as the train halted.

Rosie dropped down beside George. 'What on earth, what on EARTH were you doing?'

'I wanted to scare them away. This train is mine and Ned's. We fixed* it. It's our secret. The Bluebell is the only good thing I have, now that Dad's gone.'

Claire had run out of the shed and was standing beside the train. 'Oh George,' she said. 'Why didn't you tell me?'

16 Back on Track

Old Ned led the three children back to his cabin. He plugged in his kettle and took four mugs and an old teapot from a cupboard. 'I think we could all do with a nice cup of tea, don't you?'

'I'm sorry about smashing through the back wall of your shed,' George said, watching Old Ned wash the blood from his face with cotton wool.

'I'm sorry I brought my classmates here to hunt for ghosts,' Claire said.

'I'm sorry I took you to Mrs Harkett's for that clock,' Rosie said, looking at the floor. 'If you'd been here, none of this would have happened.'

'Now, now, there's no real damage* done,' Old Ned said. 'I'll probably have a headache for a while, but it's nothing serious.' He sat down.

'You're Edward Woodham, aren't you?' Rosie said.

Ned was surprised by the question.

'Who's Edward Woodham?' George said.

'I am,' Old Ned said. 'That's the name my mother and father gave me, although no-one uses it much anymore.'

Rosie looked at Claire and George. 'After Claire found the train, I discovered an article about a train accident. Someone had left an empty coal truck on the line and the Bluebell crashed into it.'

Old Ned shook his head. 'I was two, too young to remember.'

'Edward Woodham's mum and dad and brother were all killed in the accident.'

'That's awful,' George said.

'I was at my Granny and Grandpa's,' Old Ned said. 'I wasn't with them on the train.'

'How come you have the Bluebell now?' George asked. 'Don't you hate it?'

'It wasn't the Bluebell's fault. She and her carriage were towed* into a siding* and left. Time passed. As a boy, I used to visit it when I missed my family. A shed was built over her. And then the branch* line closed down. No one wanted to fix the Bluebell. As time passed, I grew up, and the land came up for sale. I bought it with the money left to me by my parents. That train is my connection to them, and this land is sacred* to me. It's my church.'

'But you've covered it with rubbish.' Claire said.

'Who says it's rubbish?' Old Ned said. 'This is a treasure* trove full of useful things waiting to be remade into something new. People throw too much away these days.'

'I like fixing things,' George nodded.

'It's thanks to George here that I finally got around to working on the Bluebell. I couldn't bring myself to go near her for a long time.' He smiled at George. 'You arrived here, so sad and I thought, I know what will cheer him up. I didn't know that sharing the Bluebell would cheer me up too.'

'The Bluebell is the most beautiful train in the world.' George looked at Rosie. 'Ned and I, we've been working hard to fix her.'

'And now she moves!' Rosie said.

'A bit too much!' Claire said, and they all laughed.

'Everything's OK,' Ned said.

'Apart* from your head,' George said.

'I feel terrible,' Claire bit her bottom lip. 'I should have come and asked you before bringing people to see your engine.'

'I remember what it was like being a child,' Old Ned grinned, 'Curiosity* is an important part of growing up.'

'Now, why don't we stop worrying about what's happened and decide what to do about the Bluebell.'

'What do you mean?' Rosie asked.

'Well, the engine works, but she's not ready for the public. She needs a lick* of paint, and her carriage wants new seat covers.'

'You mean we could fix her up?' Claire asked. 'Do you think we could use her as a club house?'

'Don't see why not,' Ned nodded.

'That would be wonderful!' George cried.

'I could write an article for the newspaper about her, to raise some money to pay for the paint,' Rosie said. 'I've done lots of research on the Bluebell. I could tell everyone about the train and the junkyard, and how you want us to reuse the things we throw away.'

'I'll get everybody who came ghost hunting to help us paint the train,' Claire said, 'as an apology*.'

'Do you think I could learn how to drive the Bluebell one day?' George said.

'I think I can teach you how to do that,' Old Ned smiled.

'Getting the Bluebell back on the rails is going to be a great adventure,' Rosie said, and they all agreed.

1. Auflage 1 $^{6\,5\,4\,3\,2}$ | 2025 24 23 22

© Ernst Klett Sprachen GmbH, Rotebühlstraße 77, 70178 Stuttgart 2020
Alle Rechte vorbehalten.
www.klett-sprachen.de

Autor: M. G. Leonard
Redaktion: Don Haupt
Layoutkonzeption: Maja Merz
Illustrationen: Alex Shurety
Gestaltung und Satz: Joachim Schrimm, bostext, Friolzheim
Umschlaggestaltung: Maja Merz
Titelbild: Alex Shurety

Druck und Bindung:
Plump Druck & Medien GmbH, Rheinbreitbach

Printed in Germany

ISBN 978-3-12-530903-6